"By Dauntless Resolution and Unconquerable Faith": Selected Anniversary Celebrations at the Site of the Wright Brothers' First Flight, 1928-1978

STEPHEN E. MASSENGILL

North Carolina Office of Archives and History
Raleigh
2003

ISBN 0-86526-312-4

COVER: On December 17, 1953, at the fiftieth anniversary celebration of the Wright brothers' historic flight at Kill Devil Hill, aviator Billy Parker flew his home-built Pusher biplane over the site to commemorate the event. In this photograph by Aycock Brown, from the Outer Banks History Center in Manteo, North Carolina, pioneer aviators Niels Bangs (left) and Syd Vincent observe Parker's flight. A six-foot-high granite boulder commemorating the site of the first flight in 1903 is visible in the background. " 'By Dauntless Resolution and Unconquerable Faith': Selected Anniversary Celebrations at the Site of the Wright Brothers' First Flight, 1928-1978" first appeared as an article in the October 2003 issue of the *North Carolina Historical Review*.

"By Dauntless Resolution and Unconquerable Faith": Selected Anniversary Celebrations at the Site of the Wright Brothers' First Flight, 1928-1978

STEPHEN E. MASSENGILL

> During the night of December 16, 1903, a strong, cold wind blew from the north. When we arose on the morning of the 17th, the puddles of water which had been standing about camp since the recent rains, were covered with ice. The wind had a velocity of ten to twelve meters per second (twenty-two to twenty-seven miles an hour). We thought it would die down before long and so remained indoors the early part of the morning. But when ten o'clock arrived, and the wind was as brisk as ever, we decided that we had better get the machine out and attempt a flight. . . . After running the motor a few minutes to heat it up, I released the wire that held the machine to the track, and the machine started forward into the wind. Wilbur ran at the side of the machine, holding the wing to balance it on the track. . . . Wilbur was able to stay with it until it lifted from the track after a forty-foot run. One of the life-saving men snapped the camera for us, taking a picture just as the machine had reached the end of the track and had risen to a height of about two feet.[1]

This year marks the one-hundredth anniversary of that seminal event, one of mankind's greatest accomplishments—the first successful powered flight of a heavier-than-air machine by Orville and Wilbur Wright at Kitty Hawk, North Carolina, on December 17, 1903. Perhaps the earliest celebration honoring the Wright brothers' flying achievements took place in Dayton, Ohio, in June 1909, when their hometown sponsored a homecoming event. The first memorial actually erected to honor the achievements of the Wright brothers was in France. Dedicated in 1912 in an open field at Camp d'Auvours near Le Mans, the great black granite boulder contains the brief inscription, "Wilbur Et Orville Wright Kitty Hawk, 1903." In a subsequent tribute to the Wrights, France placed a sculpted figure with arms raised up toward the sky near the cathedral at Le Mans in 1920.[2] America's oldest aeronautical magazine, *Aviation*, included in its December 17, 1923, issue an in-depth article titled "The Twentieth Anniversary of

1. Quotation from Orville Wright, "Our Early Flying Machine Developments," in *Slipstream*, January 1925, reprinted in Peter L. Jakab and Rick Young, eds., *The Published Writings of Wilbur and Orville Wright* (Washington, D.C.: Smithsonian Institution Press, 2000), 64. John T. Daniels, a crew member from the Kill Devil Hills Lifesaving Station, assisted the Wright brothers and snapped the famous photograph of the twelve-second flight.

2. Tom D. Crouch, *The Bishop's Boys: A Life of Wilbur and Orville Wright* (New York: W. W. Norton and Co., 1989), 504-505.

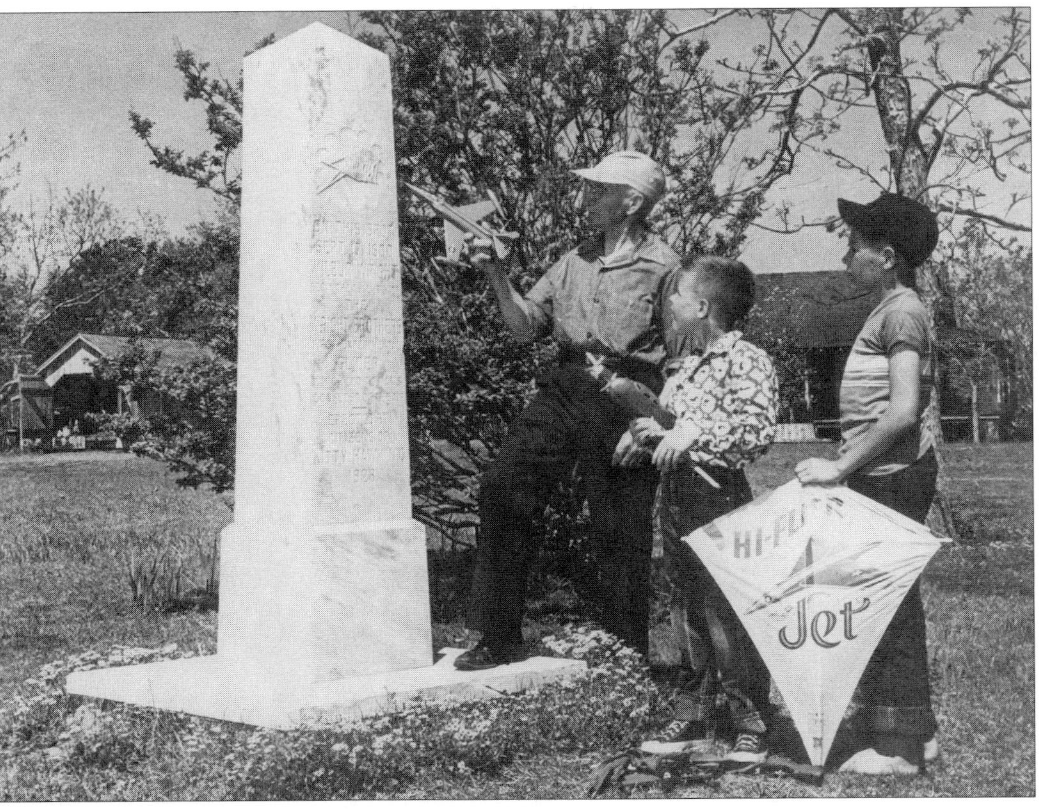

The first memorial in North Carolina to honor the Wright brothers was a five-foot marble obelisk featuring an inscription and an engraving of a Wright glider, unveiled on May 2, 1928. William J. "Bill" Tate helped raise funds to purchase the monument, which was erected in his front yard at Kitty Hawk. In this undated photograph, Elijah Baum, who led Wilbur Wright to Bill Tate's house in 1900, shows the monument to two young visitors. Photograph from the Outer Banks History Center, Archives and Records Section, Office of Archives and History, Manteo, North Carolina.

Mechanical Flight." Also in 1923, Brig. Gen. Albert J. Bowley (1875-1945), commanding general at Fort Bragg, requested that an airplane fly from Pope Field in Fayetteville to Kill Devil Hill in honor of the twentieth anniversary. Bowley got his wish, but the airship failed to land at Kitty Hawk because of fog and strong winds. The airplane, piloted by army aviator Lt. Guy Kirksey, was forced to return to Pope Field via Langley Field near Hampton, Virginia. In North Carolina, a group of citizens formed the Kill Devil Hills Memorial Association in 1927 to stage an annual observance at Kill Devil Hill on the anniversary date of the first flight. William J. "Bill" Tate (1869-1953), who had hosted the Wrights during their initial visit to Kitty Hawk in 1900, successfully raised funds for a monument to be erected by local residents. A five-foot marble obelisk featuring an inscription and an engraving of a Wright glider was placed in Tate's front yard at Kitty Hawk and unveiled on May 2, 1928, becoming the first memorial in North Carolina to honor the Wrights.[3]

On the national scene, Congress in 1927 had authorized construction atop Kill Devil Hill of a much larger memorial to honor the Wright brothers. Congressman Lindsay C. Warren (1889-1976) of North Carolina and Sen. Hiram Bingham (1875-1956) of Connecticut co-sponsored the legislation. Congress made the initial appropriation for the Wright Memorial in March 1928, and the cornerstone of the edifice was laid on the twenty-fifth anniversary of the first flight—December 17, 1928.

Beginning with the silver anniversary, national and state organizations have sponsored annual commemorations at the site, paying tribute to the Wright brothers' feat. Some of the largest and most significant commemorative celebrations held at Kill Devil Hill between 1928 and 1978 are described below.

TWENTY-FIFTH ANNIVERSARY CELEBRATION, DECEMBER 17, 1928

To celebrate the twenty-fifth anniversary of the first successful flight, the International Civil Aeronautics Conference and the National Aeronautic Association organized a pilgrimage from Washington, D.C., to Kitty Hawk. Ben Dixon MacNeill (1889-1960), a staff correspondent for the Raleigh *News and Observer*, who also documented the event with his camera, reported that more than two hundred individuals representing forty nations made the pilgrimage. Among the delegates to

3. William J. Tate, comp., *Brochure of the Twenty-Fifth Anniversary Celebration of the First Successful Airplane Flight, 1903-1928, Kitty Hawk, North Carolina, December 17, 1903* (Coinjock, N.C.: The compiler, 1928), 9. Tate distributed the souvenir publication to delegates of the International Civil Aeronautics Conference who visited the site on the twenty-fifth anniversary celebration. Tate became the leading promoter in North Carolina of the Wright brothers' flying achievements. Thomas C. Parramore, *First to Fly: North Carolina and the Beginnings of Aviation* (Chapel Hill: University of North Carolina Press, 2002), 294-295. *News and Observer* (Raleigh), December 17, 1923, May 18, 1940. The original marker was damaged in a storm and has been moved to the town hall in Kitty Hawk. A replica of the original monument was erected and still stands on Moore Shore Road. Judith A. Dempsey, *A Tale of Two Brothers: The Story of the Wright Brothers* (Victoria, Can.: Trafford Publishing, 2003), 156.

the conference, held in Washington, D.C., December 12-14, were many prominent figures in the aeronautical field, members of Congress, and cabinet officials.

At the close of the conference, the delegation, including such notables as Orville Wright, Senator Bingham, Secretary of War Dwight F. Davis (1879-1945), aviatrix Amelia Earhart (1897-1937), aeronautical engineer Igor I. Sikorsky (1889-1972), and Italian airplane builder Giovanni B. Caproni (1886-1957), departed Washington on December 15 aboard the steamer *District of Columbia* for the difficult journey to Kitty Hawk. In 1928, the Outer Banks of North Carolina was one of the most remote destinations on the East Coast, and getting there was a considerable challenge. The party arrived at Old Point Comfort in Virginia on December 16 and toured Langley Field before heading to Norfolk, Virginia. The following morning, buses transported the group to Currituck Courthouse, North Carolina. Angus W. McLean (1870-1935), governor of North Carolina, and William O. Saunders (1884-1940), president of the Kill Devil Hills Memorial Association, had welcomed and joined the party at the North Carolina-Virginia border. Automobiles replaced the buses at Currituck Courthouse because they were better suited to travel the forty miles over the main road, which was then under construction and included many detours to Point Harbor on Currituck Sound. The entourage then crossed the three-mile-wide shallow waters of Currituck Sound by ferry and proceeded the final six miles by automobile to Kitty Hawk.[4] Visitors attending the ceremony from mainland North Carolina, including newspapermen, were transported to the Outer Banks aboard the USS *Pamlico* and boats provided by the U.S. Coast Guard.[5] Several thousand visitors, mostly making their way on foot, joined the group from Washington in Dare County.[6]

The party dined on pork barbecue and turkey provided by the Kill Devil Hills Memorial Association at Virginia Dare Shores (a local establishment) and subsequently had to travel a distance of about three miles over the shifting sand to the site of the first-flight ceremony. An amusing incident occurred just prior to the festivities when Amelia Earhart, along with Reed G. Landis (1896-1975), a celebrated World War I flier and son of Judge Kennesaw Mountain Landis, commandeered a Coast Guard wagon and two horses. Tired of waiting for the few cars to transport visitors to the site, Earhart and Landis, picking up passengers along the way, guided

4. *News and Observer*, December 16, 17, 1928. Some of MacNeill's photographs are housed in the North Carolina Collection, Wilson Library, University of North Carolina at Chapel Hill, and at the Outer Banks History Center, Office of Archives and History, Manteo, North Carolina. *Twenty-fifth Anniversary of the First Airplane Flight: Proceedings at the Exercises Held at Kitty Hawk, N.C., on December 17, 1928, in Commemoration of the Twenty-Fifth Anniversary of the First Flight of an Airplane Made by Wilbur and Orville Wright*; 70th Cong., 2d sess., 1929, H. Doc. 520 (Washington, D.C.: Government Printing Office, 1929), iii-vi; Stephen Kirk, *First in Flight: The Wright Brothers in North Carolina* (Winston-Salem, N.C.: John F. Blair, Publisher, 1995), 261-262. Langley Field was named for Samuel P. Langley, airplane pioneer and rival of the Wrights.

5. *News and Observer*, December 16, 1928.

6. Kirk, *First in Flight*, 262.

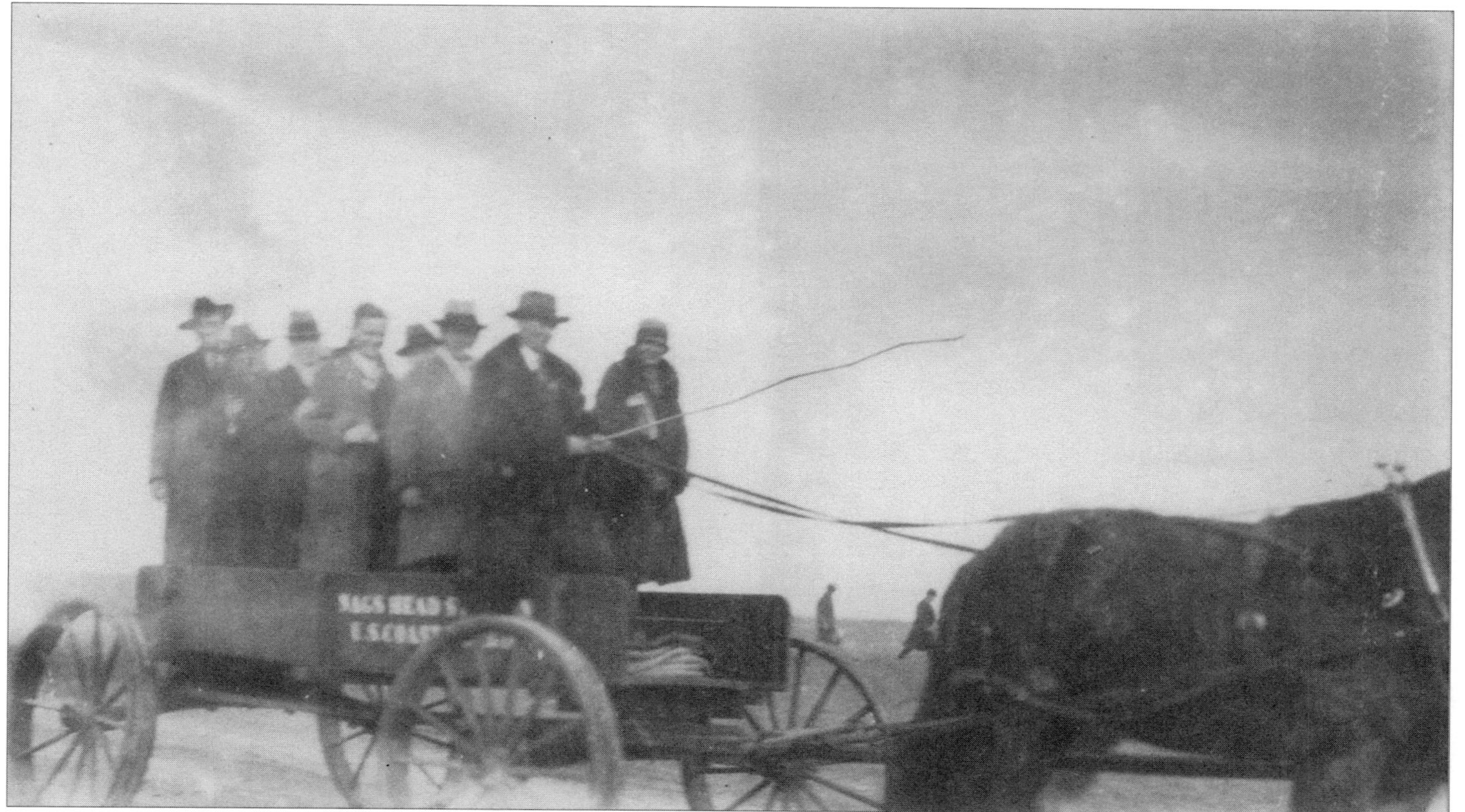

Tired of waiting for one of the few cars to transport visitors to the site of the twenty-fifth anniversary festivities on December 17, 1928, aviatrix Amelia Earhart and World War I pilot Reed G. Landis commandeered a Nags Head Coast Guard wagon and two horses. Earhart (pictured, right) and Landis picked up members of the pilgrimage from Washington, D.C., and guided the team about three miles to Kill Devil Hill. Photograph by Ben Dixon MacNeill from the North Carolina Collection, Wilson Library, University of North Carolina at Chapel Hill.

the team from the dock over the sand some three miles to the scene of the celebration.[7]

The large assemblage first gathered at a platform atop Kill Devil Hill to witness the first of two brief ceremonies—the laying of the cornerstone of the national monument. It was from this hill that the Wrights made numerous experimental glider flights during the three years leading up to the first engine-powered flight. Assistant Secretary of War F. Trubee Davison (1896-1976), who had been a pilot in World War I, presided over the event, which included a welcome by Governor McLean, an address by Congressman Warren, and the laying of the cornerstone by means of a crude derrick. Secretary of War Davis, presiding over that portion of the program, proclaimed, "Since time immemorial nations have consecrated battlefields and erected monuments to their distinguished sons. This nation, dedicated to peace, may well consecrate these sea-swept, sandy shores as a peace-time battlefield, for here mankind conquered the air." Orville Wright previously had deposited documents and descriptions of the first flight in a special box, which had already been placed in the cornerstone. Congressman Roy G. Fitzgerald of Ohio, on behalf of the citizens of Dayton, presented an American flag for the occasion. Participating in the ceremony were three of the four eyewitnesses to and assistants at the initial flights—John T. Daniels (d. 1948), Adam D. Etheridge (d. 1940), and Willie S. Dough (b. ca. 1869-d. before 1932).[8]

The crowd then moved about a half-mile down the hill to the approximate site of the first flight, where a six-foot-high granite marker, covered by a silk parachute, had been placed on a small mound. It was difficult to determine the precise site of the first flight because the nearby sand dunes had shifted some five hundred feet since 1903. Capt. Bill Tate and three of the witnesses to the first flight verified the location of the now-famous event. The National Aeronautic Association erected the marker, which was carved to resemble a boulder. Executive secretary of the National Advisory Committee for Aeronautics John F. Victory (1892-1974) presided over the unveiling of the marker. W. O. Saunders and Captain Tate addressed the crowd, and Senator Bingham, who also served as president of the National Aeronautic Association, dedicated and presided over the unveiling. The marker contained a bronze tablet with an inscription commemorating the achievement of the Wrights. Saunders laid a wreath at the foot of the boulder in honor of Wilbur Wright, who had died in 1912. That act became a tradition observed at subsequent anniversary celebrations. The modest Orville Wright did not make any public remarks. Motion-picture cameramen and newspaper staff photographers recorded the event for posterity.

7. *News and Observer*, December 18, 19, 1928.

8. *News and Observer*, December 18, 1928. Johnny Moore was the eyewitness not present at the 1928 celebration.

The crowd that came to commemorate the twenty-fifth anniversary celebration is shown ascending Kill Devil Hill to witness the laying of the Wright Memorial cornerstone. Photograph from the Outer Banks History Center.

After the cornerstone laying at the Wright Memorial during the twenty-fifth anniversary celebration, the crowd moved about a half-mile down the hill, where a six-foot granite marker was unveiled, designating the site of the first flight. Present were (right to left) Amelia Earhart, Sen. Hiram Bingham, and Orville Wright, shown standing by the marker. Photograph from the State Archives, Office of Archives and History, Raleigh, North Carolina.

It is somewhat ironic that no airplanes participated in the first commemoration. Squadrons of airships were to have come down from naval air stations in Virginia, but area duck hunters protested so strongly that the flights were canceled. Charles A. Lindbergh (1902-1972) had planned to attend the celebration but was advised by friends not to do so for fear that he would steal the limelight from Orville Wright. A year earlier, Lindbergh had gained worldwide fame for making the first nonstop solo flight from New York to Paris. Thus ended the silver anniversary celebration—the event that spearheaded the growth of the Wright brothers' memorial site.[9]

Dedication of the Wright Memorial, November 19, 1932, and the Thirtieth Anniversary Celebration, December 17, 1933

On November 19, 1932, a ceremony was held atop Kill Devil Hill to dedicate the newly completed Wright Memorial. This was the only occasion that the commemoration was not celebrated on December 17. No explanation was given as to why the ceremony was held on November 19 rather than December 17. Because the

9. *Twenty-Fifth Anniversary of the First Airplane Flight*, vi-vii; *News and Observer*, December 18, 19, 1928; Kirk, *First in Flight*, 262-263.

monument was completed in August, officials perhaps decided to schedule the ceremony early in hopes that the weather would be milder.

Before construction on the monument could begin, the ninety-foot-tall, twenty-six-acre pile of sand known as Kill Devil Hill had to be stabilized. The hill had migrated some five hundred feet since 1903, and it, along with the cornerstone, would be lost to the elements if not properly anchored. The U.S. Army Quartermaster Corps erected a fence around the base of the hill and planted vegetation on the entire dune.[10]

Work began on the monument in February 1931, and workers laid the last granite stone on August 13, 1932. The monument is supported by a concrete foundation sunk thirty-five feet into the dune and sits atop a star-shaped base that extends twelve feet into the sand. The memorial is built of white granite from Mount Airy, North Carolina, and is sixty feet high. The North Carolina Granite Corporation transported granite blocks to Norfolk, Virginia, by rail, and barges delivered the building material to the Outer Banks. The New York firm of Rogers and Poor were the architects, and the Willis, Taylor and Mafera Corporation served as building contractors. Capt. John A. Gilmer supervised the construction of the monument, a massive pylon, which cost approximately $250,000.

The inscription around the base of the monument reads: "In Commemoration of the Conquest of the Air by the Brothers Wilbur and Orville Wright, Conceived by Genius, Achieved by Dauntless Resolution and Unconquerable Faith." The memorial room on the first floor of the building initially included a model of the original airplane and a bust of each of the two brothers. A circular stairway ascends to the map room, which at the time of construction contained a display depicting all of the historic flights between 1903 and 1928. Above these rooms were a platform to house an electric panel board and an observation deck. The memorial also included a turret beacon to shine at night as a guide to shipping and aviation.[11]

Nineteen thirty-two marked Orville Wright's last appearance at an anniversary celebration at Kill Devil Hill. Surviving witnesses Adam D. Etheridge, John T. Daniels, and Johnny Moore were likewise on hand for the program. Other special guests included Bill Tate and Alpheus W. Drinkwater (d. 1962), the telegrapher who erroneously took credit for transmitting the first message about the powered flights.[12] Wright and Tate clarified the record at the 1932 dedication by confirming that Joe Dosher (b. ca. 1872), the operator of the weather bureau office at Kitty Hawk, had actually dispatched the first message about the successful flights to the Wrights' father,

10. Kirk, *First in Flight*, 263-264. The fence was erected to keep wild animals from eating the vegetation.

11. *News and Observer*, November 20, 1932. The beacon was soon removed from the top of the memorial because it confused boat captains who were not accustomed to a light at that location. During restoration of the monument that began in 1997, the beacon was repaired and is operating today. The map was in poor condition and was placed in storage, as were the original busts of the Wright brothers. The ones in front of the monument are reproductions.

12. Kirk, *First in Flight*, 161.

Construction of the Wright Memorial began in February 1931 and was completed on August 13, 1932. On November 19, 1932, a ceremony was held atop Kill Devil Hill to dedicate the sixty-foot monument. This photograph from the State Archives shows construction workers at the base of the Wright Memorial.

Bishop Milton Wright (1828-1917) in Dayton. Drinkwater did, however, telegraph the first news of the flights, which appeared in a story published by the *Norfolk Landmark* after the telegraph agency leaked the news to a reporter.[13]

Inclement weather curtailed many of the planned activities and reduced the attendance at the dedication of the memorial. A large air show planned for the event never materialized. Many airplanes were grounded at Langley Field, and the navy dirigible *Akron* could not get airborne that day. Only one navy biplane and two Coast Guard airplanes were able to fly during the ceremony. The *News and Observer* vividly described how the commemoration proceeded despite "howling winds and sweeping rain."[14]

Speaking from a pavilion specially erected for the dedication were Secretary of War Patrick J. Hurley (1883-1963), North Carolina governor-elect J. C. B. Ehringhaus (1882-1949), Congressman Lindsay C. Warren, and Gen. Louis H. Bash (1872-1952), the Acting Quartermaster General, who presided over the affair. Secretary Hurley declared, "By the eloquent monument America pays a profound tribute to two of her immortal sons. Little that we may say here today will add to the lustre of their renown or to the glory of their achievements. Far more eloquent than words, the

13. *News and Observer*, November 20, 1932; Thomas C. Parramore, *Triumph at Kitty Hawk: The Wright Brothers and Powered Flight* (Raleigh: Office of Archives and History, North Carolina Department of Cultural Resources, 2003), 79-80.

14. *News and Observer*, November 20, 1932; *Independent* (Elizabeth City, N.C.), November 18, 1932.

Orville Wright's last appearance at an anniversary celebration was at the dedication of the Wright Memorial on November 19, 1932. He is pictured here (left) with Capt. William J. "Bill" Tate, who was host to the Wright brothers in December 1903 when the first successful flight was made. It was he who suggested that the trials be held at Kitty Hawk. Associated Press photograph from the Library of Congress, Washington, D.C.

mighty aircraft that fly above us day and night proclaim their handiwork." Ruth Nichols (1901-1960), one of the world's foremost female fliers, unveiled the granite pylon while the Coast Artillery Band from Fortress Monroe, Virginia, played the national anthem.[15]

Also present for the ceremony were other notable military and government officials, including W. A. Moffatt, chief of the navy's Bureau of Aeronautics; Josephus Daniels (1862-1948), former secretary of the navy; John G. Pollard, governor of Virginia; Gen. Manus McCloskey of Fort Bragg; J. Van B. Metts, North Carolina adjutant general; and Charles G. Abbot (1872-1973), secretary of the Smithsonian Institution. At the close of the formal exercises, which were broadcast by radio for the first time, the guests attended a luncheon hosted by the Kill Devil Hills Memorial

15. *News and Observer*, November 20, 1932.

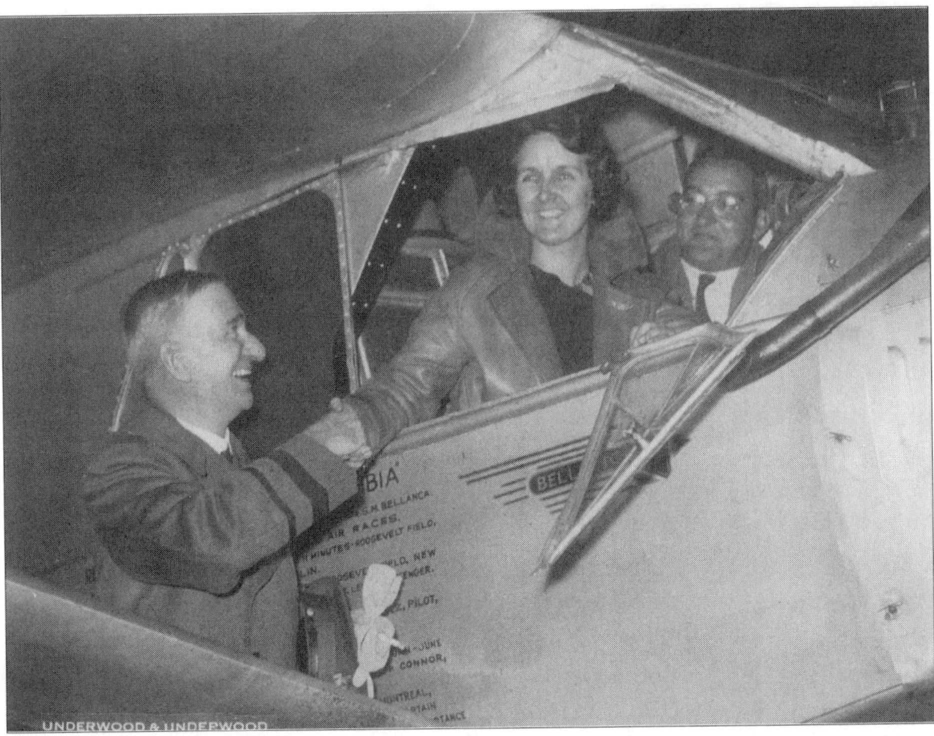

Gen. Louis H. Bash greets Ruth Nichols, one of the world's foremost women pilots, on her arrival at Washington Hoover airport in the *Columbia*, at that time the only airplane to have completed two transatlantic flights. Nichols unveiled the memorial marking the Wright brothers' first flight at the November 19, 1932, dedication ceremony. Photograph from the Library of Congress.

Association.[16] Completion of the three-mile-long Wright Memorial Bridge over Currituck Sound made travel to the 1932 event somewhat easier than in 1928.

On the thirtieth anniversary of the first flight in 1933, Orville Wright attended the dedication of the Hall of Aviation in the new Franklin Institute at Philadelphia and was the guest of honor at a civic luncheon in Dayton. Lt. Comdr. Frank M. Hawks, a well-known pilot, was scheduled to drop a wreath at the Wright Memorial in North Carolina, but dense fog in Washington, D.C., prevented him from taking off. Hawks was to have attempted to break a speed record in the flight from Washington to Kitty Hawk to Dayton and back to the nation's capital. There was no formal ceremony at the memorial. Several hundred people visited the site, and, again, witnesses Daniels, Etheridge, and Moore, as well as telegraph operator Drinkwater, gathered at the base of the pylon on a balmy and clear day.[17]

16. *News and Observer*, November 20, 1932.

17. *News and Observer*, December 17, 18, 1933.

THIRTY-FIFTH ANNIVERSARY CELEBRATION, DECEMBER 17, 1938

The weather adversely affected plans for the 1938 commemoration of the first flight. Heavy fog severely impeded visibility and grounded 182 airplanes from two large naval aircraft carriers, which were one hundred miles away and had been scheduled to pass in review at the conclusion of the formal exercises. Slated to appear was Charley Edison (1890-1969), assistant secretary of the navy and son of Thomas A. Edison, but the poor conditions prevented him from arriving at the ceremony. Orville Wright did not attend the anniversary event. Ben Dixon MacNeill, as in 1928, covered the festivities for the *News and Observer*.

On this occasion, a brief formal program took place at the base of the Wright Memorial. W. O. Saunders, one of the founders of the Kill Devil Hills Memorial Association, presided over the affair in the place of the president, A. W. Drinkwater, who apparently was not comfortable as a public speaker. Drinkwater would become a fixture at these anniversary celebrations for several decades. D. Bradford Fearing (1890-1943), president of the Roanoke Island Historical Association, presented a five-foot wreath to the two retired Coast Guardsmen and witnesses to the first flight, John T. Daniels and Adam D. Etheridge, who passed the wreath on to two of their grandchildren—Billie Cox and Jack Wilson—who together positioned it above the massive bronze doors of the memorial.

Maj. Gen. Henry H. "Hap" Arnold (1886-1950), chief of the U.S. Army Air Corps, briefly addressed the crowd. Next, Capt. P. M. L. Bellinger, commandant of the naval air station at Hampton Roads, Virginia, spoke briefly before Capt. T. L. Chalker, chief of the Coast Guard Air Service, addressed the assemblage. Following the military representatives were brief remarks by V. K. Stephenson, passenger agent for the Pennsylvania Central Airlines, and mayors George A. Isley of Raleigh, John A. Gurkin of Norfolk, and Jerome Flora of Elizabeth City. The formalities ended with a brief statement by Maj. Gen. Frank Maxwell Andrews (1884-1943), commander general of the General Headquarters Air Force.[18]

At the close of the formal program, a bomber was scheduled to fly over in commemoration of the original flight. But because of poor visibility, a weather-reporting aircraft that was in the area monitoring conditions for the military replaced the bomber and completed the flight. With no improvement in the weather, the participants left Kill Devil Hill and gathered at Roanoke Island, where they dined on duck and chicken courtesy of the Kill Devil Hills Memorial Association and the Roanoke Island Historical Association. The celebration culminated that evening with an impressive army light show in which a battery of anti-aircraft artillery searchlights bathed the memorial with more than one billion candlepower of light.[19]

18. *News and Observer*, December 16, 17, 18, 1938.

19. *News and Observer*, December 18, 20, 1938.

Poor weather dampened festivities at the thirty-fifth anniversary celebration on December 17, 1938; however, a brief formal program took place at the base of the Wright Memorial. Participating in the ceremony were (pictured, left to right) W. O. Saunders, Capt. John T. Daniels, Capt. Adam D. Etheridge, Capt. P. M. L. Bellinger, and Mayor John A. Gurkin of Norfolk, Virginia. Photograph from the State Archives.

* * *

The 1943 ceremony to honor the fortieth anniversary of the first flight was canceled as a result of heavy snow across eastern North Carolina. Maj. Gen. Thomas Hanley Jr., commander of the U.S. Army Air Force Eastern Flying Command at Maxwell Field, Alabama, was one of a few military personnel to arrive in Dare County. He made a brief address to a small group of naval men at the auxiliary air station at Manteo because the party was unable to reach Kill Devil Hill.[20]

Forty-Fourth and Forty-fifth Anniversary Celebrations, December 17, 1947 and 1948

The forty-fourth anniversary of the Wright brothers' first flight featured a gathering of the rotary-wing aircraft industry in Dare County. The helicopter took center stage at the event, along with its Russian-born inventor, Igor I. Sikorsky, who had been present at the initial anniversary celebration. The formal exercises at the

20. *News and Observer*, December 17, 18, 1943.

Helicopters took center stage at the forty-fourth anniversary celebration on December 17, 1947. Speakers at the event included (pictured, left to right) William T. Daniels, Gov. J. Melville Broughton, and Igor Sikorsky, the Russian-born inventor of the helicopter. Photograph from the State Archives.

memorial were again simple. The Elizabeth City High School Band provided music for the occasion and entertained a crowd estimated to be the largest since the laying of the memorial's cornerstone in 1928. More than two hundred navy fighter planes flew over the memorial in a salute, followed by twelve Bell army jet fighters. Next, three helicopters, one transporting Sikorsky, approached the site. A Bell and a one-seater Bendix landed at the foot of the hill, and a Sikorsky, bearing its namesake, landed near the crest of the hill. Sikorsky was then escorted to the base of the pylon. There he joined the other guests for the traditional wreath laying by four grandchildren of the four Coast Guardsmen who were present at the first flight in 1903. Other special guests included former governor J. Melville Broughton (1888-1949), who served as North Carolina's chief executive during World War II, A. W. Drinkwater, and Capt. John T. Daniels, who was making his final appearance at an anniversary event. Afterward, the three helicopters amused the crowd with demonstrations of their maneuverability and agility in the sky. The flight of the smaller Bendix, piloted by Dare County resident Dave Driskill, especially delighted the gathering. A Coast Guard search-and-rescue team performed a simulated rescue, and later, some two hundred people gathered at the annual luncheon at the Carolinian Hotel at Nags Head to hear Sikorsky pay tribute to the Wright brothers.[21]

Dual ceremonies were held on the forty-fifth anniversary of the first flight in December 1948—at Washington, D.C., and at Kill Devil Hill. Orville Wright had died on January 30, 1948. In Washington, his nephew, Milton Wright, formally presented the original airplane, the *Kitty Hawk*, to the Smithsonian Institution before a crowd of six hundred government, military, and aircraft industry officials. Representing North Carolina were Johnny Moore, the last surviving witness, Bill Tate, and D. Victor Meekins (1897-1964), chairman of the Dare County Board of Commissioners. In a message to the secretary of the Smithsonian, President Harry Truman welcomed the arrival of the airplane: "No more fitting repository for this historic plane could be found. . . . It will quicken in all hearts an appreciation of the achievements of American inventive genius."[22]

A typical simple ceremony took place at the memorial in North Carolina. Following the wreath-laying ritual, a painting titled *The First Flight*, by artist Melbourne Brindle (1904-1995), was unveiled and immediately flown to Washington to be exhibited at the commemoration in the nation's capital. The six hundred people who gathered at the memorial later witnessed an air show that included blimps, helicopters, amphibious planes, fighter planes, and jets. Assistant Secretary of the Navy Mark E. Andrews was the keynote speaker at the luncheon.[23]

GOLDEN ANNIVERSARY CELEBRATION, DECEMBER 14-17, 1953

Joint sponsors of the fiftieth anniversary celebration included the Kill Devil Hills Memorial Society (previously known as the Kill Devil Hills Memorial Association), the Air Force Association, the National Park Service, and the Fiftieth Anniversary of Powered Flight Commission. Gov. William B. Umstead (1895-1954) had appointed the nine-member commission with Carl Goerch (1891-1974) as chairman. The commission decided to make the celebration a four-day affair instead of a one-day observance as in the past. It was the most elaborate of the many worldwide celebrations planned to commemorate the first flight. The event was an ambitious undertaking, given the remoteness of the site, with no airport and a location fifty-eight miles from the nearest airline and fifteen miles from the nearest telegraph office.

The four-day commemoration was divided into the following themes: December 14: Pioneers and Flyers Day; December 15: Industry Day; December 16: Defense Day; and

21. *News and Observer*, December 17, 18, 1947.

22. *News and Observer*, December 17, 18, 1948.

23. *Program Commemorating Forty-Fifth Anniversary First Flight, Wright Memorial, Kill Devil Hills, North Carolina, December 17, 1948*, Outer Banks History Center; Parramore, *Triumph at Kitty Hawk*, 95, 98-99. The historic aircraft had been on display at the Science Museum in London since 1925. Word came from Washington, D.C., on December 17, 1943, that the airplane would return to the United States after the war.

December 17: Anniversary Day. The National Park Service reconstructed and refurnished the Wright brothers' 1903 hangar and living quarters. In addition, pilot Billy Parker, sales representative for Phillips Petroleum Company, reenacted the first flight in his 1912 Pusher biplane at approximately the same time as the actual event had occurred.

During the mid-December activities, more than two hundred aircraft demonstrated the progress of modern aviation. Six F-86 Sabrejets broke the sound barrier as they streaked past the historic site. A Royal Air Force Canberra jet bomber arrived at the memorial from London and dipped its wings in honor of the Wrights. In further tribute, a National Airlines Douglas DC-7 flew over the memorial at four hundred miles per hour following its record-setting flight from Los Angeles to Washington. The "Thunderbirds," a U.S. Air Force jet aerobatic team, thrilled the crowd with a fifteen-minute demonstration of precision maneuvers by four F-84 Thunderjets flying no more than five feet apart at more than five hundred miles per hour.[24]

Windy and rainy weather canceled most of the flying portion of the first day's program on December 14 and greatly reduced attendance. Officials dedicated the reconstructed living quarters and hangar, and granddaughters of the witnesses laid the traditional wreaths at the base of the memorial. None of the participants or eyewitnesses were still alive, but the widows of John T. Daniels and Adam Etheridge were present. Special guests included Mrs. Henry H. Arnold, A. W. Drinkwater, and retired brigadier general and pioneer flier Frank P. Lahm (1877-1963), president of the Kill Devil Hills Memorial Society. Twenty aviation pioneers from Oklahoma, including Billy Parker, were likewise on hand.[25]

A flag-raising ceremony conducted on a windy and chilly morning at the memorial was one of the highlights of "Industry Day" on December 15. Brigadier General Lahm raised the flag of the United States; Admiral Dewitt C. Ramsey, president of the Aircraft Industries Association, raised the flag of the United Nations; and Edward O. Rodgers, assistant to the president of the Air Transport Association, raised the International Goodwill Flag. Admiral Ramsey and Rodgers next laid wreaths at the foot of the monument and in the afternoon addressed the industry luncheon at the Carolinian Hotel.[26]

24. *Golden Anniversary Observance of Man's First Successful Powered Flight: Proceedings at the Exercises Held at Wright Brothers National Memorial, December 14-17, 1953, in Commemoration of the Fiftieth Anniversary of the First Flight of an Airplane Made by Wilbur and Orville Wright*; 83rd Cong., 2d sess., 1954, H. Doc. 480 (Washington, D.C.: Government Printing Office, 1954), ix, x, xiii, 1-4, 23; *Guide to Research Materials in the North Carolina State Archives: State Agency Records* (Raleigh: Division of Archives and History, North Carolina Department of Cultural Resources, 1995), 785.

25. *News and Observer*, December 15, 1953. Lahm had become the second army airplane pilot when the Wright brothers taught him to fly in 1909.

26. *News and Observer*, December 16, 1953; *Golden Anniversary Observance*, 2.

The fiftieth anniversary celebration (December 14-17, 1953) was the most elaborate of the many worldwide events planned to honor the first flight. Over two hundred aircraft demonstrated the progress of modern aviation, including the "Thunderbirds," a U.S. Air Force aerobatic team of F-84 Thunderjets, shown here flying in formation near the Wright Memorial. Photograph from the State Archives.

An impressive aerial review, held before a crowd of two thousand people, ended the morning session of "Defense Day" on December 16. Participants in the air show included the U.S. Marine Corps, Army, Air Force, and Coast Guard (Elizabeth City Air Station), the Air Force "Thunderbirds," and Bensen Aircraft of Raleigh. Four-star general J. K. Cannon, commander of the Tactical Air Force; Rep. Herbert C. Bonner (1891-1965); and Mrs. Leontine Wright Jameson, niece of the Wright brothers, were among the dignitaries who witnessed the show from the first-flight reviewing stand.[27]

Some five thousand spectators watched an awe-inspiring display of air power on Anniversary Day, December 17. James H. "Jimmy" Doolittle (1896-1993), retired general and chairman of the National Fiftieth Anniversary Committee, spoke at the morning outdoor session and at a luncheon held at the Carolinian Hotel:

> When the Wrights had finished their work in 1903 and had packed up their improbable-looking plane and closed camp to go back to Ohio, the air was no more buoyant than before, and the Atlantic was just as wide as ever. Yet because of the Wrights' work, the oceans have shrunk—in time—and the continents have been joined through the air. . . . In a few decades, aviation has changed our lives. With the aid of modern aircraft, we can transport ourselves, the goods of peace, and the instruments of war over great distances at high speeds. The airplane has greatly stimulated the growth of our

27. *Golden Anniversary Observance*, 3; *News and Observer*, December 17, 1953.

economy, and it has been the vital element in assuring our security—in preserving our freedom. . . . It is good that aviation has gained so firm a place in the life of the Nation. It should be remembered that aviation has won its place because it has progressed so fast, adapted itself so well to the needs of the times, and anticipated so well the requirements of the future. This progress must be continued. It must be accelerated.[28]

Lt. Gov. Luther H. Hodges (1898-1974) was also present at the luncheon and spoke on behalf of Governor Umstead, who was unable to attend. At the historic moment (approximately 10:35 A.M.), Billy Parker took off in his 1912 home-built Pusher biplane in a stiff wind and circled around markers indicating where the Wrights had made their first four flights. Parker flew his aircraft at an altitude of about one hundred feet, considerably higher than the Wright Flyer in 1903. Subsequently, performances featuring modern aircraft, including the aforementioned British Canberra jet bomber, the National Airlines DC-7, and the "Thunderbirds," entertained the gathering.[29] Some fifteen thousand individuals attended the golden anniversary celebration of flight in Dare County. North Carolina received worldwide publicity during the four-day event from radio, television, motion-picture newsreel, and newspaper coverage. And in 1953, the official name of the National Park Service historic site became the Wright Brothers National Memorial.

* * *

A new $275,000 National Park Service visitor center and administration building was dedicated during the fifty-seventh anniversary commemoration. A small crowd attended the December 17, 1960, ceremony, which occurred in the wake of two tragic airplane crashes—one in New York and the other in Munich, Germany. Maj. Gen. Benjamin D. Foulois (b. ca. 1884), a pioneer aviator and chief of the U.S. Army Air Corps from 1931 to 1935, made the principal address at the Wright Memorial. He had been present at its dedication in 1932. The festivities included the traditional wreath laying by grandchildren of the witnesses to the first flight, as well as a fly-over by some of the most modern aircraft of the Air Force. Gov. Luther H. Hodges spoke briefly at the dedication of the new building, and Governor-elect Terry Sanford (1917-1998) spoke at the luncheon. Other notables present for the occasion were Rep. Herbert C. Bonner, Lindsay C. Warren, Outer Banks historian David Stick, and A. W. Drinkwater.[30] It may have been the last celebration attended by the telegrapher, who died of cancer in 1962.[31]

28. *Golden Anniversary Observance*, 20.

29. *Golden Anniversary Observance*, 4; *News and Observer*, December 18, 1953.

30. *News and Observer*, December, 17, 18, 1960. The Wright Brothers' Memorial Visitor Center was officially opened to the public on July 15, 1960. The interior of the Wright Memorial, which had served as the visitor center from 1932 until the completion of the new building, was closed to the public.

31. Kirk, *First in Flight*, 304.

Among the highlights at the fiftieth anniversary celebration was Billy Parker's reenactment of the Wright brothers' first four flights in his 1912 home-built Pusher biplane. Parker circled around markers indicating where the Wrights had made their first flights, reaching an altitude of about one hundred feet. This postcard photograph of Parker in his biplane also includes an inset photograph of the pilot. Postcard courtesy of the author.

SIXTIETH ANNIVERSARY CELEBRATION, DECEMBER 16-17, 1963

On December 15, 1963, the night before the sixtieth birthday celebration of the first flight, astronaut and Ohio native John H. Glenn (b. 1921) was warmly welcomed at the annual meeting of the Man Will Never Fly Memorial Society. This unusual social organization was formed in 1959 to pay tribute to the doubters in the early twentieth century who refused to believe that the Wright brothers would ever get their machine off the ground. The group meets each year prior to the anniversary celebration to reaffirm—during a lengthy cocktail party—its belief that man cannot fly.[32]

The sixtieth anniversary celebration was a two-day affair held on December 16 and 17. On the morning of the first day, Glenn moderated a panel discussion during a flight seminar for young people attended by student delegates from twenty states. The internationally known pilots who served on the panel included Jacqueline Cochran (ca. 1906-1980), world-famous pilot and business executive; Maj. Robert A. Rushworth (1924-1993), pilot of the U.S. Air Force experimental jet X-15; James Nields, industry president and business pilot; Lieutenant Colonel Glenn, Project Mercury astronaut; TWA captain emeritus Hal Blackburn, jet pilot; and Max Conrad, record-setting flier.

32. *News and Observer*, December 17, 1960, December 16, 1963.

At the sixtieth anniversary celebration in 1963, held on December 16 and 17, astronaut John H. Glenn moderated a panel discussion during a fight seminar for young people. He is shown here examining a model of the Wright brothers' airplane in the visitor center at Kill Devil Hill. Photograph from the State Archives.

In the afternoon officials gathered at the visitor center to dedicate a replica of the Wright Flyer. Conrad L.Wirth (1899-1993), director of the National Park Service, remarked that his organization had made an unsuccessful attempt to persuade the Smithsonian Institution to donate the authentic Wright Flyer to the site. During the afternoon program, visitors witnessed the traditional placement of memorial wreaths, as well as flying demonstrations. Secretary of Commerce and former governor Luther H. Hodges addressed more than three hundred people at the Monday-night banquet held at the Carolinian Hotel, delivering his comments less than a month after the death of John F. Kennedy.[33] "Kitty Hawk," he said, was a

> testing ground for the dream of flight . . . so now this nation is a testing ground for dreams of universal brotherhood. . . . With this new understanding, we should have a somewhat clearer insight into the historic mission of our country. We are more aware that the United States of America was not created by destiny solely for its citizens to enjoy life, liberty, and the pursuit of happiness. We feel anew that this nation was created for a larger purpose, to advance freedom, justice, and equality for men of all nationalities, all races, all creeds, and for all time to come.[34]

33. *News and Observer*, December 16, 17, 1963; *Program of Events, The 60th Anniversary of Powered Flight Observance, Kitty Hawk Area, North Carolina, December 16-17*, Outer Banks History Center.

34. *News and Observer*, December 17, 1963.

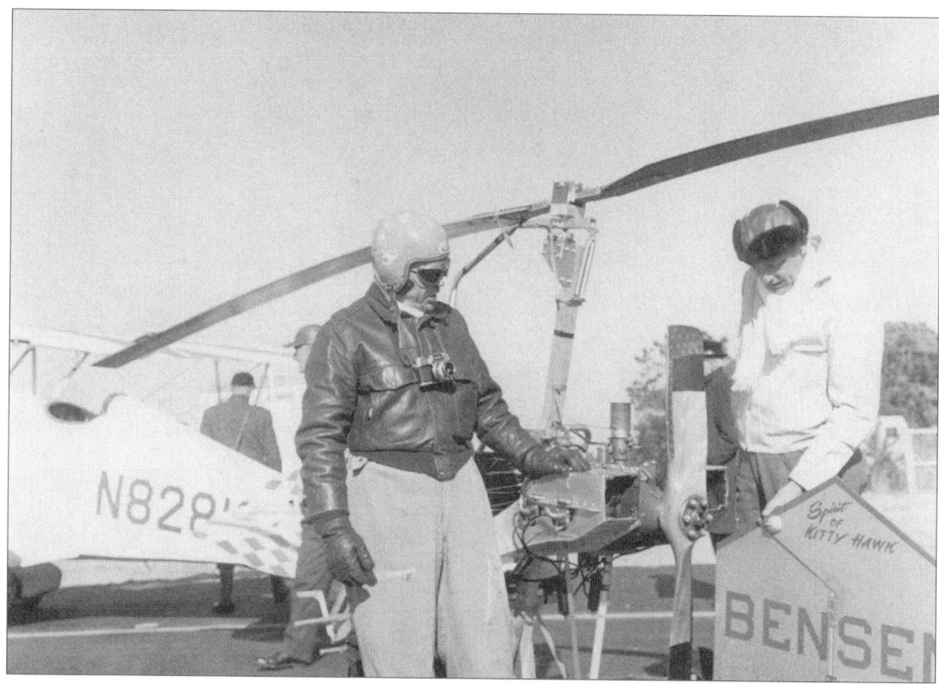

More than seventy aircraft, representing all five branches of the military service, were featured in a dazzling air display at the sixtieth anniversary celebration. Igor Bensen (left) of Raleigh is shown here with his Gyro-Copter, *Spirit of Kitty Hawk*, made by Bensen Aircraft Corporation. Photograph from the State Archives.

The main event on the agenda for the December 17 birthday observance of flight was the dedication of a three-thousand-foot paved landing strip for small aircraft, which had been constructed adjacent to the takeoff path used by the Wrights on the day of the successful flights. Gov. Terry Sanford was the main speaker for the event. A unique ribbon-cutting ceremony occurred when a twin-engine airplane with Hodges and Sanford aboard sliced the ribbon as the aircraft took off from the runway. United States senator A. S. (Mike) Monroney (b. 1902), chairman of the Senate Subcommittee on Aviation, spoke to the gathering of some three hundred people, who braved the cold but clear day. A dazzling air display by more than seventy aircraft representing all five branches of the military service capped off the two-day commemoration. The Air Force "Thunderbirds" performed their famous aerial maneuvers after flying in from Dayton, Ohio. The *Spirit of Kitty Hawk*, a one-man Gyro-Copter made by Bensen Aircraft Corporation of Raleigh, made a demonstration flight for the crowd.[35]

35. *News and Observer*, December 18, 1963.

SEVENTY-FIFTH ANNIVERSARY CELEBRATION, DECEMBER 11-17, 1978

The First Flight Society (prior to 1966 known as the Kill Devil Hills Memorial Association/Society) and the National Park Service sponsored the diamond anniversary celebration. The seven-day (December 11-17) schedule began with a first-flight educational program for the general public and school groups. Individual sessions focused on the story of the Wright brothers and the development of aviation between 1903 and 1978. On Saturday, December 16, Paul E. Garber (1899-1992), historian emeritus of the Smithsonian Institution, and Charles Gibbs-Smith, Lindbergh Professor of Aerospace History at the National Air and Space Museum, Smithsonian Institution, made an entertaining presentation titled, "The Real Orville and Wilbur Wright."[36]

A crowd of six thousand enthusiastic spectators gathered for the main program on December 17. Addressing the crowd were U.S. Attorney General Griffin B. Bell (b. 1918), U.S. Transportation Secretary Brock Adams (b. 1927), and U.S. Assistant Secretary of the Interior Robert L. Herbst. Past president of the First Flight Society Lorimer W. Midgett (1911-1980) presided at the ceremony. John R. Allison, president of the National Aeronautic Association, was present to rededicate the granite marker that his organization had placed at the site fifty years earlier to denote the precise point of departure of the first successful flight. Continuing a practice that began in 1928, descendants of the Wright brothers and the witnesses placed memorial wreaths at the boulder-shaped marker.

The majority of the throng had come to see Ken Kellett, of the organization Quest for Flight, attempt to reenact the historic first flight. The twenty-five-year-old resident of Boulder, Colorado, constructed a replica of the Wright Flyer from plans provided by the Smithsonian Institution. Kellett, who was dressed in a turn-of-the-century suit, almost duplicated the feat on his third attempt. The front of the airplane lifted off the wooden track for a few seconds, but the tail dragged behind and never lifted off the rail. Apparently, the 550-pound airplane did not have a strong enough head wind to become airborne. Moments later, four F-105 Thunderchief fighter-bombers of the 192d Tactical Fighter Group, Virginia Air National Guard, roared overhead in a thunderous salute to the Wright brothers. The Sea Fare Restaurant at Nags Head hosted the annual luncheon of the First Flight Society. Sen. John H. Glenn, who was unable to attend the function, was inducted into that organization's hall of fame.[37]

36. *Seventy-fifth Anniversary Program of the First Powered Flights of a Heavier-Than-Air Flying Machine by Orville and Wilbur Wright Which Took Place on December 17, 1903*, Outer Banks History Center.

37. *Program of the Seventy-fifth Anniversary*; *News and Observer*, December 17, 18, 1978; *Raleigh Times*, December 18, 1978.

Six thousand spectators gathered at the seventy-fifth anniversary celebration, held on December 17, 1978. Most had come to see Ken Kellett reenact the Wright brothers' historic flight. Kellett nearly duplicated the event on his third try but was unable to get his "Wright Flyer" fully airborne. Photograph of Kellett's attempted reenactment from the Outer Banks History Center.

In the early 1990s, the North Carolina Office of Archives and History acquired a full-scale reproduction of the Wright brothers' Flyer from Kellett Aviation. It is currently on display at the North Carolina Museum of History in Raleigh.

The celebrations honoring the achievement of the Wright brothers discussed here were mostly well-planned affairs executed by hardworking local, state, and national organizations. The 1928 (twenty-fifth), 1953 (fiftieth), and 1978 (seventy-fifth) anniversary celebrations attracted the largest crowds. Of course, these were landmark years and included special programs and dignitaries to commemorate the event. Although the activities surrounding the program have expanded in scope over the years, the plans have retained some of the traditional activities—notably the laying of memorial wreaths; music by local high school bands; flying demonstrations; addresses by high-ranking officials in the military, governmental, and aeronautical fields; appearances by officials from Ohio and members of the Wright family; and luncheons hosted by the First Flight Society and its predecessors. The celebrations saluted past exploits of the Wrights and at the same time examined the advancement of aviation. All of the celebrations had to endure the possibility of adverse weather conditions on the Outer Banks in mid-December. Furthermore, event planners had to face the problems of staging a celebration in such a remote location.

The worldwide activities surrounding the one-hundredth anniversary of the first successful powered flight by a heavier-than-air machine promise to be the most extensive and varied during any time in history. During 2003, events have been scheduled throughout the United States to commemorate the Wright brothers' contribution. Planners of the North Carolina event on the Outer Banks, scheduled for December 12-17, no doubt will borrow ideas from former programs to ensure that the new agenda will have a connection to the past. The one-hundredth-anniversary celebration should be an outstanding event and will likely be one of the largest of its kind ever held in the state. The ubiquitous cameras and camcorders carried by the news media and other visitors to the event should well document the one-hundredth birthday festivities and leave a large body of visual records for future generations.

NOTE ON PHOTOGRAPHS

Surprisingly, I located many excellent photographs taken at the major anniversary celebrations held in North Carolina between 1928 and 1978. The public sources included the Library of Congress, the North Carolina State Archives, the North Carolina Collection at the University of North Carolina at Chapel Hill, and the Outer Banks History Center. The State Conservation and Development, Travel and Tourism photographs, and the *News and Observer* photographs at the State Archives were especially rich collections. A nice group of photographs by Ben Dixon MacNeill is housed at the North Carolina Collection. Two important groups of images by Aycock Brown and the Dare County Tourist Bureau form part of the holdings of the

Outer Banks History Center. Sisters Rebecca Drane Warren of Chapel Hill and Frances Inglis of Edenton shared with me snapshots of the 1928 event taken by their father, Frederick Blount Drane (1890-1982), an Episcopal clergyman in Edenton. Drane, who as a boy spent his summers on the Outer Banks, had on several occasions hunted for relics of the Wright flights. He found a wing tip half buried in the sand and later a control lever in an abandoned hangar. Drane kept the souvenirs for about twenty-five years before returning them to the Smithsonian in 1933. He was rewarded for the deed by Orville Wright, who sent him a piece of wing fabric and a wood chip from damaged pieces of the original Wright Flyer that flew on December 17, 1903.

Mr. Massengill is the iconographic archivist at the North Carolina State Archives and the author of Photographers in North Carolina: The First Century, 1842-1941, *forthcoming from the Office of Archives and History.*

INDEX